BLISTER BEETLE

ATLAS MOTH

LITTLE KIDS FIRST BIG BOOK OF BUGS

BY CATHERINE D. HUGHES

NATIONAL GEOGRAPHIC KiDS

WASHINGTON, D.C.

CONTENTS

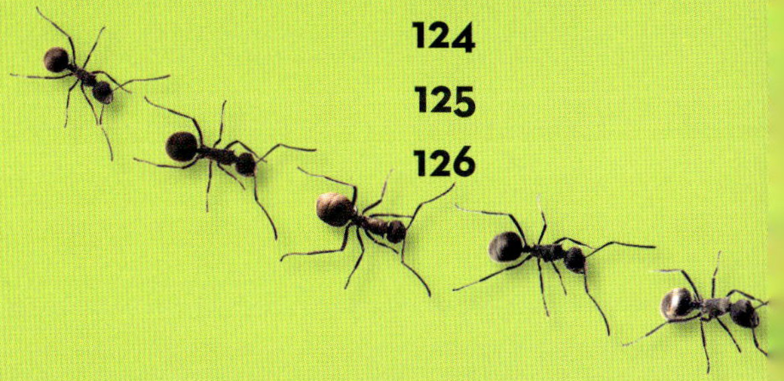

INTRODUCTION

This book introduces a selection of insects and a few other kinds of "bugs." It answers questions from "What is an insect?" and "How do bees make honey?" to "Are spiders insects?" and "Where do cicadas live?" The first chapter introduces the topic of insects. Each of the next six chapters features insect species that share behavioral or anatomical characteristics. The last chapter highlights a few bugs that are not insects, such as spiders and earthworms.

NATIONAL GEOGRAPHIC'S *LITTLE KIDS FIRST BIG BOOK OF BUGS* IS DIVIDED INTO EIGHT CHAPTERS:

CHAPTER ONE

begins the book with a look at what makes a bug an insect. Sequences of photographs show examples of insects going through complete and incomplete metamorphosis. A fun photo game that reinforces topics in the chapter wraps up this and each subsequent chapter.

CHAPTER TWO

introduces social insects, including ants, bees, and wasps. Readers will get inside views of a leaf-cutter ant nest and honeybee hive. Photo galleries show a few of the many other species of ants, bees, and wasps.

CHAPTER THREE

explores the world of beetles. From ladybugs to fireflies, beetles represent the largest group of insects, and this chapter celebrates the huge variety.

CHAPTER FOUR

shimmers with butterflies, moths, and their caterpillars. Colorful photo galleries and a game reinforce the wide range of species.

CHAPTER FIVE

touches on a few of the more annoying, pesky insects: flies, fleas, and mosquitoes.

CHAPTER SIX

takes readers leaping, hopping, and crawling with grasshoppers, crickets, and mantises.

CHAPTER SEVEN

introduces cicadas, stick insects, and dragonflies.

CHAPTER EIGHT

treats readers to a few popular "bugs" that are not insects. Fascinating spiders, other arachnids, and the familiar earthworm and roly-poly bring readers to the end of the book.

HOW TO USE THIS BOOK

Colorful **PHOTOGRAPHS** illustrate each spread, supporting the text. Galleries showcase the diversity of species for several groups of insects.

FACT BOXES for each featured species give the young reader a quick overview including range, diet, number of young, predators, its type of metamorphosis, and its size compared with a five-year-old child's hand.

Interactive **QUESTIONS** in each section encourage conversation related to the topic.

MORE FOR PARENTS In the back of the book you will find parent tips, with fun activities that relate to bugs, and a helpful glossary.

POP-UP FACTS sprinkled throughout provide added information about bugs featured in each section.

A **GAME** at the end of each chapter reinforces concepts covered in that section.

CHAPTER 1

WONDERFUL BUGS!

ASIAN SWALLOWTAIL CATERPILLAR

The world is full of animals, including insects and other bugs. In this chapter, discover what makes an animal an insect.

WHAT IS A BUG?

LADYBUG

Bugs are animals.

The word **"BUG"** can mean any creepy-crawly creature—from a spider or worm to an insect such as a bee or a cricket.

Animals include mammals (you are a mammal!), birds, reptiles, amphibians, fish, and invertebrates.

Invertebrates are animals that do not have a backbone. Bugs are invertebrates.

SPIDER

WORM

INSECTS are the largest group of invertebrates. Most of this book is about insects. The last chapter is about other kinds of creepy-crawlies.

An insect usually has six legs that are jointed, or can bend. Every insect has three main body parts—a head, a thorax, and an abdomen. An insect has two antennae—body parts on its head that the insect uses to smell or to feel. Some insects even hear with them.

Most adult insects have wings and can fly.

Most insects hatch from eggs. Some kinds, such as butterflies, do not look at all like their parents when they hatch.

These insects go through a big change called **COMPLETE METAMORPHOSIS** before they look like an adult.

A BUTTERFLY LAYS HER EGG ON A PLANT.

WHEN AN EGG HATCHES, OUT POPS A CATERPILLAR! THE PLANT IT HATCHES ON BECOMES FOOD FOR THE CATERPILLAR.

A butterfly **PUPA** is also called a **CHRYSALIS.**

WHEN IT IS BIG ENOUGH, THE CATERPILLAR STOPS EATING. NOW IT BECOMES A PUPA.

SPECIAL CHANGES HAPPEN INSIDE THE PUPA. SLOWLY THE CATERPILLAR TURNS INTO A BUTTERFLY.

3

THE HUNGRY CATERPILLAR EATS AND EATS, AND GROWS AND GROWS.

6

FOR THIS MONARCH BUTTERFLY, THE CHANGES TAKE ABOUT TWO WEEKS.

7

THE BUTTERFLY BREAKS OUT OF ITS PUPA. IT STRETCHES OUT ITS NEW WINGS AND FLIES AWAY.

There are more than a **MILLION** different species, or kinds, of insects.

Other kinds of insects, such as grasshoppers, look like tiny copies of their parents as soon as they hatch from their eggs. The change these insects go through as they get bigger is called **INCOMPLETE METAMORPHOSIS.**

1

THE FEMALE TWO-STRIPED GRASSHOPPER LAYS HER EGGS IN THE GROUND.

2

THE EGG HATCHES. OUT POPS A NYMPH!

3

AS IT EATS AND GROWS, THE NYMPH GROWS NEW SKIN THAT FITS ITS BIGGER BODY. ITS OLD SKIN FALLS OFF. THIS IS CALLED MOLTING.

How many zeroes are in a million (1,000,000)?

LET'S PLAY A GAME!

How many insects can you find? Circle them with your finger.

HINT: Insects have **6** legs.

HINT: Spiders have **8** legs.

1

2

3

4

5

6

ANSWERS: INSECTS—1, EUROPEAN WASP; 3, TRUE WEEVIL; 5, SCARAB BEETLE; 6, KATYDID; 8, FUNGUS BEETLE; 9, STINK-BUG; 11, PREDACEOUS KATYDID; 13, GREEN SHIELD BUG; 14, RAINBOW SHIELD BUG. SPIDERS—2, GOLDEN SILK ORB WEAVER SPIDER; 4, WOLF SPIDER; 7, VENOMOUS WANDERING SPIDER; 10, GOLDEN ORB WEAVER; 12, WOLF SPIDER

7

8

9

10

11

12

13

14

CHAPTER 2

BUSY INSECTS

HONEYBEES

Some insects live alone. Others live together and are called social insects. In this chapter you meet a few social insects.

One leaf-cutter ant colony can have **TEN MILLION** workers.

A leaf-cutter ant can lift something that weighs **50 TIMES** what the ant weighs. That would be like you lifting two big motorcycles.

LEAF-CUTTER ANT

These busy ants grow food like farmers do.

A large group of ants, called a colony, lives in an underground nest. Each leaf-cutter ant has a job to do, and each ant is the right size for its job.

All species of ants are **SOCIAL** insects.

Do you have any jobs to do at home?

An ant colony has a queen. She is the only ant that lays eggs.

A colony also has a few males, or boys. They are a little smaller than the queen.

The different types of ants in a colony—from queens to workers—are called CASTES.

The adult queen and the males are the only ants in the colony that grow wings.

There are about **20,000 SPECIES** of ants.

Most of the rest of the colony's ants are workers. They are females, or girls. Workers are smaller than the soldier ants that guard the colony.

Media and maxima workers have strong jaws. They cut pieces of leaves from plants and carry them back into the nest.

The tiniest workers are called minima workers.

They take care of the garden where the ants grow their food, called fungus.

Fungus grows on the pieces of leaves that the medias and maximas bring into the nest.

FACTS

HOME
forests and farmland in much of Central and South America

FOOD
fungus

EGGS
30,000 in a day

PREDATORS
anteaters, armadillos, birds, flies

METAMORPHOSIS
complete

SIZE

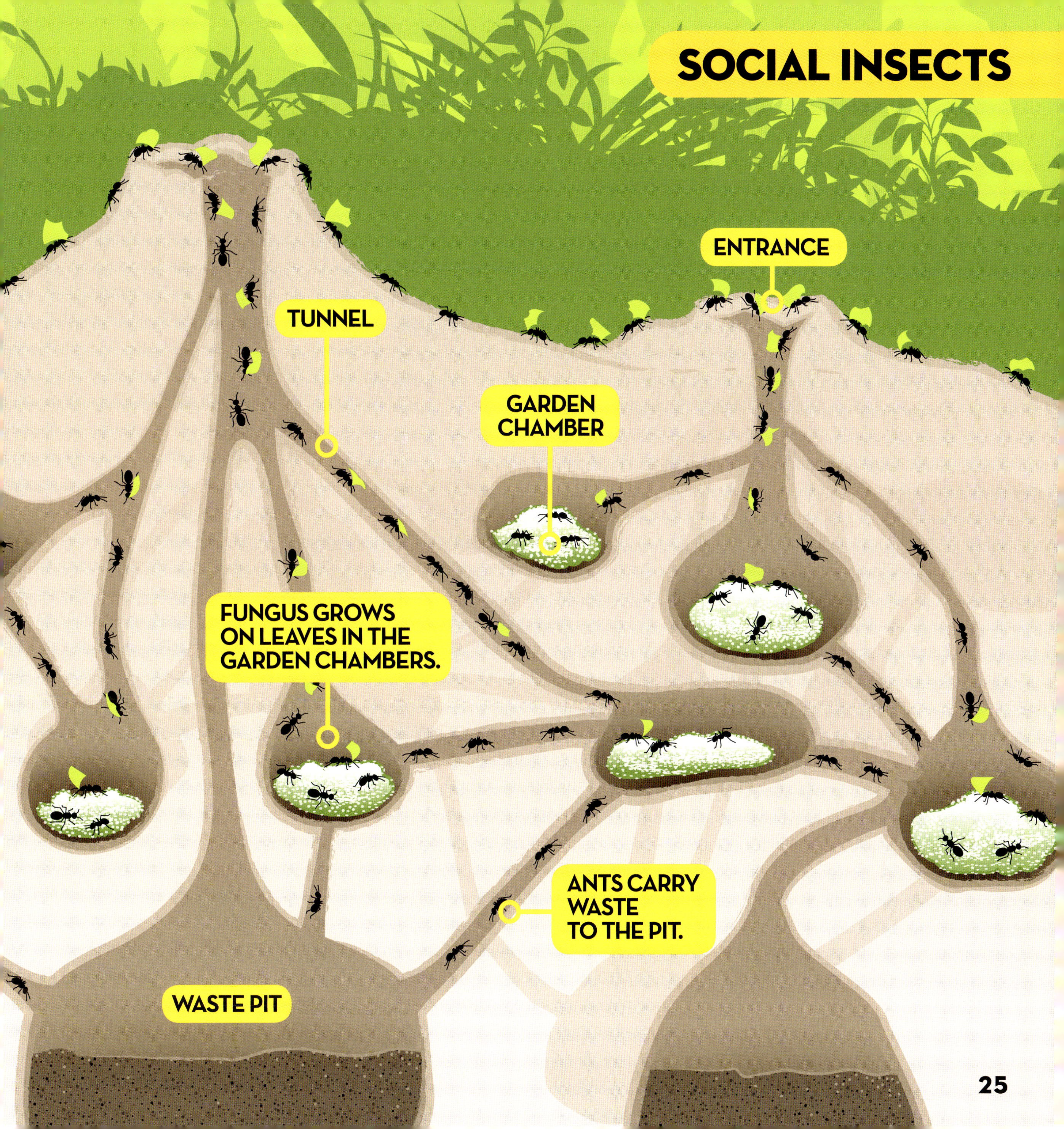
ENTRANCE
TUNNEL
GARDEN CHAMBER
FUNGUS GROWS ON LEAVES IN THE GARDEN CHAMBERS.
ANTS CARRY WASTE TO THE PIT.
WASTE PIT

ARMY ANT

Huge groups of these ants march together through the rain forest.

FACTS

HOME
forests in much of Central and South America

FOOD
tarantulas, scorpions, and insects such as cockroaches and crickets

EGGS
thousands at a time

PREDATORS
birds, giant anteaters

METAMORPHOSIS
complete

SIZE

As big groups of army ants move through the rain forest, they collect insects and other small creatures to eat.

The ants march for 15 days at a time. Then they make a nest made entirely of ants—themselves!—called a bivouac.

SOCIAL INSECTS

Sometimes the army ants cannot get across a space without a bridge. Some of the ants make a living bridge. These ants hang on to each other while other ants crawl over them.

One colony may have **TWO MILLION** ants.

So many army ants move through the rain forest at once that you can **HEAR THEM MARCHING.**

Have you ever walked across a bridge?

Ants live in many places on Earth. Most ants are black or red. Here are just a few of the more than 20,000 species of ants.

The **JUMPING ANT**, which lives in India, could jump across this open book in just five leaps.

LITTLE BLACK ANTS are common in the United States. They make nests in dirt outside, but they may come into people's houses looking for food.

CRAZY ANTS got their name from the way they behave. They run fast all over the place, rather than in a straight line.

BULLDOG ANTS are big, have large jaws, and live in Australia.

WEAVER ANTS live in leafy nests they make in trees. They live in Australia and Asia.

HONEYBEE

These insects make yummy sweet honey.

Honey comes from honeybees. The bees make honey from nectar—a sweet liquid that they find inside flowers.

A worker bee sips nectar from flowers. She carries nectar back to her hive.

The honeybee spits out the nectar to fill honeycomb cells. By now, the nectar has started to change to honey.

Have you ever tasted honey?

The bees store the honey to eat and to feed their larvae. People use honey collected from beehives to sweeten food.

FACTS

HOME
throughout most of the world wherever flowers grow

FOOD
pollen, nectar, honey

EGGS
1,000 each day; 200,000 in a queen's lifetime

PREDATORS
spiders, toads, opossums, birds, bears, and more

METAMORPHOSIS
complete

SIZE

As a honeybee collects nectar, she flies from flower to flower. Bits of pollen, a powder in flowers that helps make seeds, stick to her body.

The honeybee pushes some of the pollen into special bags on her legs called pollen baskets. It is food for hungry larvae back in the hive.

The honeybee visits other flowers, where some pollen falls off her body. This is how bees help plants make fruit and seeds so that new plants grow. Bees are important pollinators—animals that carry pollen from plant to plant.

A worker honeybee has a **STINGER** inside the end of her body. She uses it to protect the hive from enemies, and can only sting one time.

Honeybees help many plants grow. Watermelons, cucumbers, and strawberries all need honeybee pollinators.

There are three kinds of bees in each beehive: the **QUEEN,** which lays the eggs; the **DRONES,** which are the males; and the **WORKERS,** which are the females that do the work.

BEES SHOWN ACTUAL SIZE!

WORKER

longer wings than drones

QUEEN

longer and slimmer than workers

DRONE

bigger abdomen and big eyes

The honeybee is one of 20,000 different species of bees. Here are just a few other kinds of bees.

The **NEON CUCKOO BEE** sneaks into another kind of bee's nest to lay its eggs there.

The fuzzy **BUFF-TAILED BUMBLEBEE** has long, soft hair.

The **EASTERN CARPENTER BEE** is a large bee. It makes its nest in wood.

The **ORCHID BEE** is shiny green.

SWEAT BEES can be annoying to humans and other animals because they like to drink sweat.

The **SUGARBAG BEE** from Australia doesn't sting.

GOLDEN PAPER WASP

This insect makes its own kind of paper to build its nest.

Paper wasps build **NESTS** in trees and near the roofs of buildings.

What do you use paper for?

A queen wasp starts building a new nest. She hunts for little pieces of wood from logs or fences.

She chews and chews, mixing the wood with her saliva. That turns it into a paste that she spits out onto a surface. When it dries, it is paperlike and strong.

SOCIAL INSECTS

The queen makes small, six-sided cells attached to one another. She lays eggs in the cells.

Later, her daughters help make the nest bigger and bigger. The growing colony of paper wasps has a nice big home!

FACTS

HOME
woodlands and grassy open areas in much of North America

FOOD
larvae: small insects; adults: nectar

EGGS
up to 200 at a time

PREDATORS
foxes, rats, mice, birds

METAMORPHOSIS
complete

SIZE

There are about 30,000 different kinds of wasps. Some live in groups and some live alone. Here are just a few species of wasps.

The **TARANTULA HAWK** is a large wasp that hunts tarantula spiders to eat.

The **POTTER WASP** hunts for caterpillars to feed its young.

A female **GALL WASP** lays her eggs on plant leaves. The plant grows a round covering called a gall around the larva when it hatches. The gall protects the larva.

EASTERN YELLOW JACKETS like to eat sweets, such as nectar, but they feed meat to their larvae.

LET'S PLAY A GAME!

Help the honeybee, leaf-cutter ant, and paper wasp each get back to the right nest. Follow the correct path with your finger.

HONEYBEE

LEAF-CUTTER ANT

PAPER WASP

NEST

NEST

NEST

CHAPTER 3

BAZILLIONS OF BEETLES

COMMON EASTERN FIREFLIES

Beetles make up the biggest group of insects. Almost half of all insect species are beetles.

BEETLES

There may be millions of beetle species.

There are 400,000 kinds (that is a lot!) of beetles that scientists have found and named. There may be millions that have not been found yet.

Most beetles have two pairs of wings.

The front pair of wings is called the elytra. The elytra are like a shell—they protect the rest of the beetle's body, including its other pair of wings.

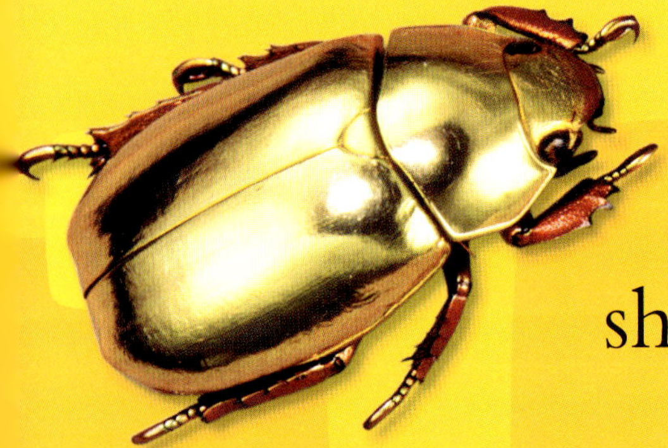

Most other insects do not have this protection. Scientists call beetles Coleoptera, which means wings with sheaths—hard coverings that protect.

BEETLES live everywhere except in the ocean and around the North and South Poles.

SEVEN-SPOTTED LADYBUG

Ladybugs are beetles.

Farmers like seven-spotted ladybugs because they eat aphids. Aphids are insects that eat crops—the plants that farmers grow.

A ladybug lays her eggs near aphids or other plant-eating insects. When the larvae hatch, they start eating the aphids around them.

LADYBUGS are also called LADY BEETLES and LADYBIRDS.

Have you ever been to a farm?

FACTS

HOME
deserts, grasslands, forests, marshes in Europe, Asia, and North America

FOOD
insects, pollen

EGGS
10-50 at a time

PREDATORS
birds, spiders, small mammals

METAMORPHOSIS
complete

SIZE

When attacked by a predator such as a bird, a ladybug releases a liquid that tastes bad.

The next time that bird goes after a ladybug, the insect's bright color is a reminder: "Leave me alone. I taste bad!"

LARVAE HATCHING

There are about 5,000 species of ladybugs. Many are red with black spots. Others are yellow or orange, and some have no spots. Here are just a few.

The **HALLOWEEN LADY BEETLE** sometimes sneaks inside people's houses to stay warm in the winter.

There are a few species of ladybugs that eat crops instead of pesky insects. This **MEXICAN BEAN BEETLE** is one.

The **YELLOW-SHOULDERED LADYBIRD** lives in Australia and New Zealand.

The **LARGE LEAF-EATING LADYBIRD** eats the leaves of some crops, such as tomatoes and potatoes.

TRANSVERSE LADYBIRDS eat many different insects that attack farmers' crops.

The **TWO-SPOTTED LADYBIRD** has one spot on each red elytron.

Another name for the common eastern firefly is the **BIG DIPPER FIREFLY.**

FACTS

HOME
near streams in meadows or woodlands, in the eastern half of the United States

FOOD
insects, worms, snails, slugs

EGGS
500 at a time

PREDATORS
another species of firefly

METAMORPHOSIS
complete

SIZE

COMMON EASTERN FIREFLY

This insect makes its own light.

The common eastern firefly is the one that you are most likely to see in the United States. You may see fireflies flashing their lights on summer evenings after dinner and before bedtime.

This insect—also called a lightning bug—uses light to "talk" to other fireflies. It makes the special light called bioluminescence inside its body. The end of its abdomen can light up.

When a male firefly wants to find a female firefly, he flies near the ground while he flashes his light every six seconds.

On the ground, a female knows that the male is the same species of firefly that she is. She answers his flashing by turning on her light. Then the male finds her.

Firefly pupae glow.

There are about **2,000** different species of **FIREFLIES.**

Have you ever caught a firefly?

IF YOU CATCH A FIREFLY, WATCH IT FOR A LITTLE WHILE, AND THEN LET IT GO.

GIRAFFE WEEVIL

GIRAFFE WEEVILS live on trees called giraffe beetle trees.

A very long neck gave this weevil its name.

This insect was only discovered in **2008.**

Weevils are beetles that have long snouts, or "noses." The male giraffe beetle has a long snout and a long neck. Females have shorter necks.

Male weevils use their long necks to fight each other. The female weevil chooses the winner to be her mate.

A female giraffe weevil uses her neck to help roll a leaf into a tube. She snips pieces of leaves with her jaws and uses her neck and legs to roll up the tip of the leaf. Then she lays her egg inside the tube, which keeps the egg safe until it hatches.

FACTS

HOME
Madagascar, an island country in Africa

FOOD
leaves of the giraffe beetle tree

EGGS
one at a time

PREDATORS
none known

METAMORPHOSIS
complete

SIZE

Were you born before or after the giraffe beetle was discovered?

LET'S PLAY A GAME!

Many beetles have names that describe what they look like or something they do. Can you match each beetle's description to its photograph?

1. **RHINOCEROS BEETLE:** This insect's horn reminds people of rhinoceroses. It is one of the strongest insects.

2. **GOLIATH BEETLE:** One of the largest insects, this beetle eats mostly fruit and tree sap, a juice that flows through the inside of trees.

3. **RED MILKWEED BEETLE:** Milkweed is a plant. It is the only thing that this beetle eats. It is also called a longhorn beetle because of its long antennae.

4. **DUNG BEETLE:** It shapes dung, or animal waste (poop), into balls. The beetle's larvae will hatch in the dung and eat it.

5. **GOLD BEETLE:** The way sunlight bounces off the elytra gives this insect a shiny golden color.

6. **BLUE FUNGUS BEETLE:** This brightly colored beetle eats fungus such as mushrooms.

ANSWERS: 1-C; 2-E; 3-A; 4-B; 5-F; 6-D

B

C

D

A

E

F

CHAPTER 4
FANTASTIC FLIERS

MONARCH BUTTERFLY

Butterflies and moths are closely related. Scientists call them Lepidoptera, which means wings with scales.

WHICH IS WHICH?

Take a peek at two similar insects.

Most butterflies fly around during the day. Most moths fly at night. Butterflies have knobs on the ends of their two antennae. Moth antennae have no knobs and some are shaped like feathers.

The scales on the wings of butterflies and moths reflect light in different directions like lots of tiny mirrors. That gives the insects their many colors.

Let's take a closer look at a few butterflies and moths.

BLUE MORPHO BUTTERFLY

Bright blue and big, this is one of the largest butterflies.

As it flies through the rain forest, the morpho flaps its wings up and down.

Bright blue color shows as the butterfly's wings flap down. The blue almost disappears when its wings flap up. That is because the undersides of its wings are brownish.

The morpho's entire life lasts only about 115 DAYS.

Can you flap your arms up and down as if you were a morpho butterfly?

FACTS

HOME
tropical forests from Mexico to Colombia

FOOD
larvae: leaves; adults: juices of rotten fruit, fungus, decaying animals, tree sap, wet mud

EGGS
one at a time

PREDATORS
birds and insects

METAMORPHOSIS
complete

SIZE

Rotting fruit makes a yummy meal for a morpho. The butterfly unrolls its proboscis—a mouthpart that is a long hollow tube. It uses it like a straw to sip juice from the fruit.

There are about 20,000 species of butterflies. Male and female butterflies often look different. Here are a few examples, along with their caterpillars.

MALE

CATERPILLAR

RAJAH BROOKE'S BIRDWING

Australia and parts of Asia

FEMALE

BUTTERFLIES & MOTHS

ADONIS BLUE
Europe

ORANGE-BANDED SHOEMAKER
Central and South America

ISABELLA TIGER MOTH

The woolly bear caterpillar turns into this moth.

FACTS

HOME
meadows, fields, prairie, woods throughout much of North America

FOOD
larvae: many plants; adult: does not eat

EGGS
several hundred eggs at a time

PREDATORS
bats, birds, spiders, wasps, flies

METAMORPHOSIS
complete

SIZE

Tiger moth caterpillars, also called woolly bears, are more famous than the moths they turn into.

Woolly bears are commonly seen in the fall. They are fuzzy, black at each end, and brown in the middle.

The adult moth lives **FOUR TO FIVE DAYS.**

This amazing caterpillar freezes all the way through its body during cold winters.

In the spring, it thaws and is still alive! It has a special kind of antifreeze in its body that keeps it alive.

In places where winters are long and very cold, a woolly bear may live through as many as **14 WINTERS** before it becomes a moth.

The Isabella tiger moth is active at night, when it flies around looking for a mate.

Can you name all the black or brown things you can see from where you are sitting?

There are about 160,000 species of moths. Here are a few of the world's moths.

The **ELEPHANT HAWK MOTH** feeds at night, sipping nectar from honeysuckle and other flowers.

The **COMET MOTH** is also called the Madagascan moon moth.

The **ATLAS MOTH** is one of the largest moth species. It can grow so big it would almost cover this book.

The **MORGAN'S SPHINX MOTH** drinks nectar deep inside flowers called orchids. It uses its very long proboscis to reach inside.

LET'S PLAY A GAME!

Can you match each caterpillar to its moth or butterfly?

You can find all of them on the pages in this chapter.

ANSWERS: A-2; B-1; C-4; D-3

C

3

2

4

D

CHAPTER 5

INSECTS THAT BUG US

COMMON GREEN BOTTLE FLIES

Some insects are pests and can be annoying. You can get to know flies, fleas, and mosquitoes in this chapter.

COMMON HOUSEFLY

This pest lives all around the world.

Houseflies do not bite or sting people. But they can carry germs that make people sick.

Fly larvae are called maggots.

Maggots hatch less than a day after the eggs are laid.

Have you ever been annoyed by flies?

They spend a lot of time in garbage and even in animal manure, or poop. These places are where flies pick up germs.

Sometimes germs get stuck on a fly's leg hairs. Then it carries those germs to wherever it lands next, including on people's food.

Flies do not have teeth. A housefly uses its saliva to soften food. Then it uses its mouth to suck up the food.

FACTS

HOME
wherever people live

FOOD
garbage, animal waste (poop), and rotting plants and meat

EGGS
up to 500 at a time

PREDATORS
wasps, fire ants, beetles, mites, spiders, birds, bats

METAMORPHOSIS
complete

SIZE

Flies eat and fly around during the **DAY** and rest at night. Flies in houses often **REST** on ceilings.

FLIES ON GARBAGE

DOG FLEA

Fleas can jump farther than almost any other insect.

FACTS

HOME
mostly on dogs, but also cats and other animals

FOOD
blood

EGGS
20 at a time; 600 over a lifetime

PREDATORS
fire ants, nematodes (small worms that eat flea larvae)

METAMORPHOSIS
complete

SIZE

Fleas' bodies are tough and hard to squash.

A flea has long hind legs that help it jump really far in one leap.

Dog fleas can make dogs very itchy. That's because fleas feed on dogs' blood. As they do, it bothers the dogs' skin.

Fleas are skinny, which helps them zoom fast through a dog's fur. Long jumps and speedy crawling help fleas escape an itchy dog's scratching paws.

Fleas are parasites. A parasite lives on another animal and gets its food from that animal's body.

How far can you jump in one leap?

You could leap over a 20-STORY BUILDING if you had a flea's leaping strength.

TIGER MOSQUITO

Mosquitoes drink blood.

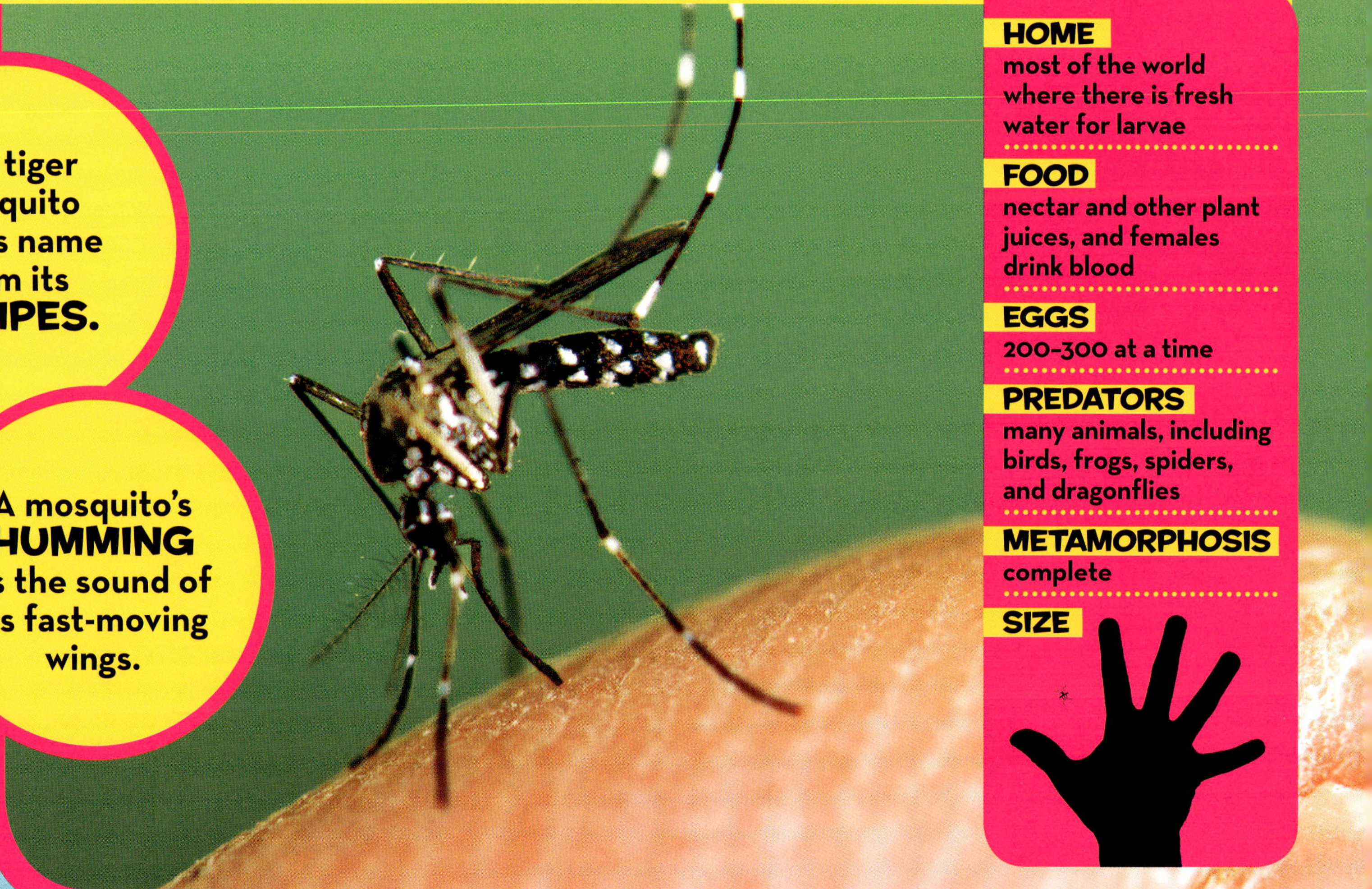

The tiger mosquito got its name from its **STRIPES.**

A mosquito's **HUMMING** is the sound of its fast-moving wings.

FACTS

HOME
most of the world where there is fresh water for larvae

FOOD
nectar and other plant juices, and females drink blood

EGGS
200–300 at a time

PREDATORS
many animals, including birds, frogs, spiders, and dragonflies

METAMORPHOSIS
complete

SIZE

A mosquito pokes its proboscis—a sharp tube on its head—into the skin of its victim and sucks up blood like you suck drinks through a straw.

There are more than 3,000 species of mosquitoes. Maybe the best thing about them is that they are food for other animals, including bats, frogs, and spiders.

Only females drink blood, and only when they are ready to lay eggs. The rest of the time, they feed on nectar and other sweet plant juices, just as the male mosquitoes do.

Have you ever had a mosquito bite?

Originally from Asia, the **TIGER MOSQUITO** has spread around the world.

LET'S PLAY A GAME!

Pesky fleas get scratched off, while mosquitoes and flies become food. Join the action by counting!

Can you count how many blue fleas the dog has scratched off?

How many orange mosquitoes is the bat going to catch?

Count how many purple flies the bird will eat.

CHAPTER 6

HOPPERS AND HUNTERS

PRAYING MANTIS

Now you will discover three fun insects: a grasshopper, a cricket, and a praying mantis.

EASTERN LUBBER GRASSHOPPER

Yellow, orange, and red colors mark this pretty grasshopper.

This big, colorful grasshopper walks or jumps to get around. It has four short wings but cannot fly.

Lubber grasshoppers spread their wings and make a loud hissing noise to scare off any enemies. They also make a smelly, bubbly liquid that tastes bad if something attacks them.

Lubber nymphs are almost completely **BLACK**. They molt five times, becoming more **COLORFUL** each time.

NYMPH

ADULT

Lubbers let each other know where they are by making a noise called stridulating (STRIH-joo-late-ing). They make the noise by rubbing their front wings against their hind legs.

FACTS

HOME
lawns, weedy fields, and woods in the southern United States

FOOD
grass, weeds, and other plants

EGGS
up to 50 at a time

PREDATORS
shrikes (a kind of bird)

METAMORPHOSIS
incomplete

SIZE

What are some ways that you make noise?

SNOWY TREE CRICKET

When you hear a cricket chirping, it is probably this kind.

People who make movies often use recordings of the snowy tree cricket in the parts of the story that take place in the summer.

That's because this cricket's chirping is heard in most of the United States in the summertime.

FACTS

HOME
shrubs, vines, and trees throughout most of the United States

FOOD
aphids, other insects, plant parts, fungus

EGGS
hundreds at a time

PREDATORS
birds, flies

METAMORPHOSIS
incomplete

SIZE

Listening carefully, scientists can tell what the temperature is outside by how fast or how slowly a snowy tree cricket chirps. The warmer it is, the faster they chirp.

Mother crickets make tiny holes in the **BARK OF TREE** branches to lay their eggs.

The female **SNOWY TREE CRICKET** lays her eggs in the fall.

Eggs **HATCH** in the spring.

Nymphs molt up to **12 TIMES** by midsummer.

This cricket lives about a **YEAR.**

Can you chirp like a cricket?

PRAYING MANTIS

Mantises can turn their heads to look behind them.

FACTS

HOME
shrubs and trees in meadows, gardens, and fields in much of the world

FOOD
crickets, grasshoppers, flies, moths

EGGS
100 at a time

PREDATORS
bats, birds, frogs, spiders

METAMORPHOSIS
incomplete

SIZE

No other insect can turn its head around like a mantis. A praying mantis can look behind it without turning its body. It just turns its head.

A praying mantis gets its food by staying still. Its green body blends in with the green plants around it, keeping it hidden.

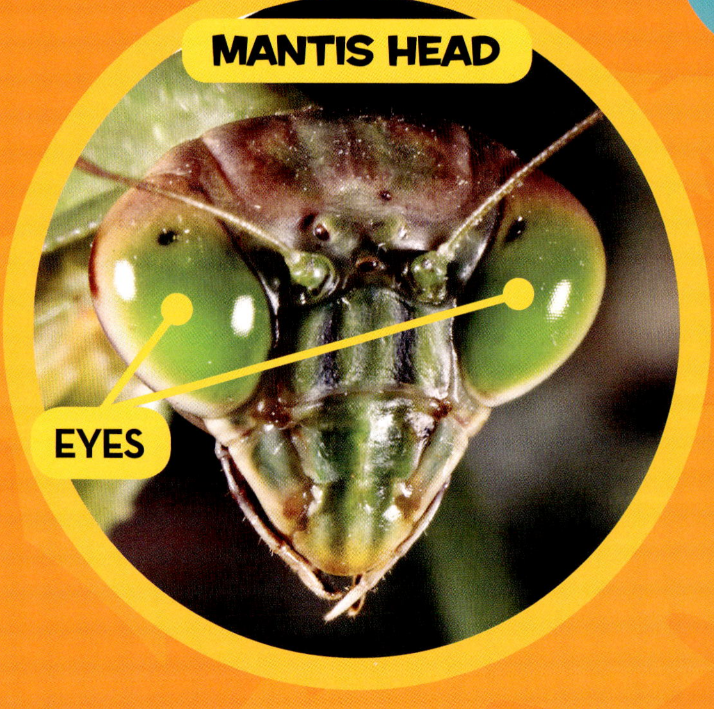

Praying mantises help farmers by **EATING INSECTS** that eat their crops.

A mantis lives for about one year.

Have you ever played hide-and-seek?

The praying mantis looks like it is praying when it is sitting still. It holds its front legs in front of its body.

When a cricket or other insect comes by, the hidden mantis grabs it with its front legs. The legs are spiky, making it hard for its prey to squirm away.

There are more than 2,300 species of mantises around the world. Here are a few of them.

CONEHEAD MANTIS

This mantis has a crest on its head that gives it the name conehead.

MALAYSIAN ORCHID MANTIS

Holding still on a flower called an orchid, this mantis hides by looking like it is part of the flower.

SPINY FLOWER MANTIS

To scare away attackers, the flower mantis rears up suddenly to look like a bigger insect with huge eyes.

GIANT DEAD LEAF MANTIS

To hide, this mantis pretends it is a dead leaf. It even rocks back and forth slowly as if the wind is blowing it.

LET'S PLAY A GAME!

Use the pictures to help you read this story about exploring.

A  and a  took a walk through a . The children smelled  with their 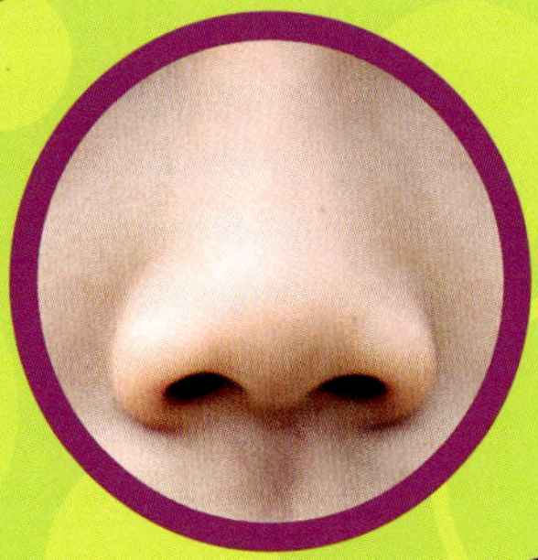s. They used their s to watch a  climb a blade of grass.

Listening with their 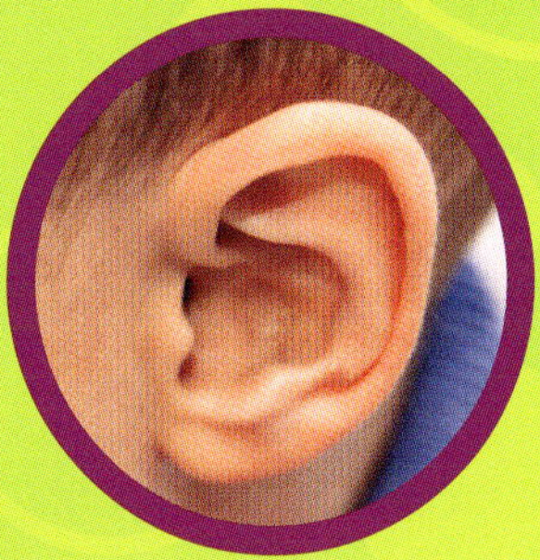 s, they heard a  chirping. A  crawled across their 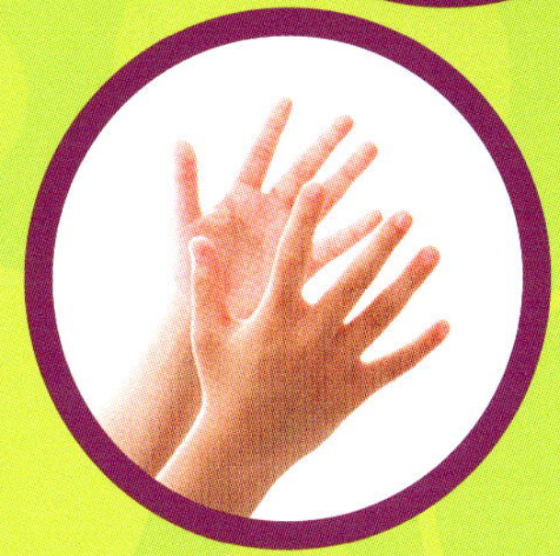 , making them giggle because it tickled. Then it was time to run back to the  where they had a delicious  with their parents. It was a fun day of exploring!

CHAPTER 7

HIDERS AND FLIERS

SOUTHERN HAWKER DRAGONFLY

Take a peek at cicadas, stick insects, and dragonflies in this chapter.

17-YEAR CICADA

For years, this cicada disappears underground.

The **NYMPHS** generally dig their way out from underground in **MAY.**

When these cicadas hatch, the nymphs tunnel into the ground. They stay there for 17 years, sucking juices from tree roots.

Then, all at the same time, thousands of nymphs crawl to the surface. They climb up into trees and shrubs.

Has anyone in your family seen 17-year cicadas come out of the ground?

FACTS

HOME
forests and other wooded areas of the eastern United States

FOOD
larvae: root sap;
adult: tree sap

EGGS
up to 500 in a lifetime

PREDATORS
birds, spiders, snakes, squirrels

METAMORPHOSIS
incomplete

SIZE

The nymphs molt one last time, crawling out of their old shell-like skin, called an exoskeleton.

Now they are adults with wings.

Some people **EAT** cicadas, and many say they **TASTE** like asparagus.

GOLIATH STICK INSECT

This big insect is life-size in the picture below.

FEMALE Goliath stick insects are bigger than **MALES.**

EVEN MORE INSECTS

Male Goliath stick insects can **FLY,** but females cannot.

The Goliath stick insect is shaped like a stick—long and skinny. Its shape and color help it hide from birds and other animals that might want to eat it.

Goliath stick insects live high up in the treetops.

During the day a stick insect stays still. It looks like part of the tree it rests on. At night, the stick insect moves around and eats.

FACTS

HOME
eastern Australia

FOOD
leaves of plants such as eucalyptus and acacia

EGGS
several hundred at a time

PREDATORS
opossum and other mammals, birds, lizards

METAMORPHOSIS
incomplete

SIZE

Have you ever climbed up a tree?

SOUTHERN HAWKER DRAGONFLY

Dragonflies can catch insects in midair with their legs.

Southern hawkers fly over water searching for small insects to eat. They spend a lot of time near ponds and streams.

Dragonflies cannot walk well on land, but they are expert fliers.

They have two pairs of wings. They can fly forward, backward, and sideways and can even hover in one spot.

A dragonfly can eat **HUNDREDS** of mosquitoes in one day.

Southern hawker nymphs **HATCH UNDERWATER.** They live there for up to three years.

FACTS

HOME
Europe, near ponds and rivers, also in woods and gardens

FOOD
adults: insects; nymphs: tadpoles, small fish, aquatic insects

EGGS
100 to 400 at a time

PREDATORS
birds, spiders, frogs, toads

METAMORPHOSIS
incomplete

SIZE

Have you ever seen a dragonfly?

There are more than **5,000** species of dragonflies.

Dragonflies sometimes eat while they are flying. Other times they land on a plant to eat.

LET'S PLAY A GAME!

Can you guess which two of these insects are cicadas, which are stick insects, and which are dragonflies? Say the missing part of each insect's name.

LARGE BROWN _ _ _ _ _ _

SCARLET _ _ _ _ _ _ _ _ _ _

EVEN MORE INSECTS

WALKING _ _ _ _ _ INSECT

EMERALD _ _ _ _ _ _ _

KEELED SKIMMER _ _ _ _ _ _ _ _ _

PRICKLY HAANIELLA _ _ _ _ _ INSECT

CHAPTER 8

BUGS—NOT INSECTS

JUMPING SPIDER

Some of the animals people call bugs are not insects. This chapter is about spiders and other non-insects.

ORB WEAVER SPIDER

The orb weaver spins a web to trap insects.

FACTS

HOME
near open fields, in tall vegetation, on houses in much of North America

FOOD
insects

EGGS
300–1,400 at a time

PREDATORS
wasps, birds, lizards

SIZE

The orb weaver spider **BUILDS ITS WEB** from two to eight feet off the ground.

Spiders have two main body parts. (Insects have three main body parts, remember?) No spiders have wings.

Spiders are arachnids. They have eight legs. (Insects have six legs, remember?)

This spider does not hurt people.

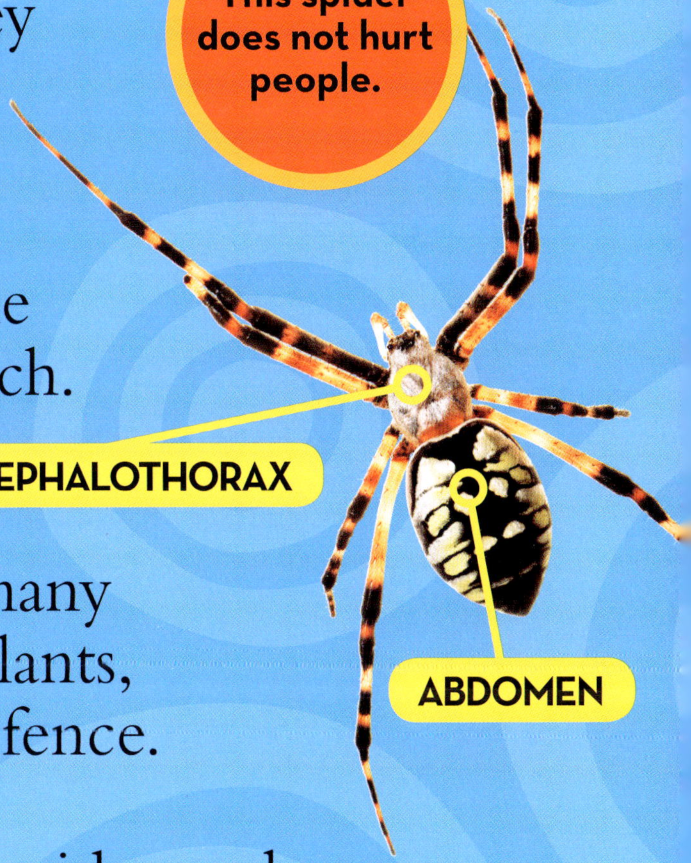

Spiders called orb weavers are one group you can easily find and watch. Just look for their spiderwebs.

Orb weavers spin their webs in many places—between trees or other plants, in the corner of a porch, or on a fence.

The web is made of silk that the spider makes inside its body. The web traps insects. Then the spider eats them.

Can you draw a picture of an orb weaver's web?

Even if you can't see it, there is almost always a spider nearby. There are at least 35,000 species of spiders. Here are just a few.

A **WOLF SPIDER** does not make a web. It waits at the opening to its burrow and pounces on insects that crawl by.

The world's largest spider is the **GOLIATH BIRD-EATING TARANTULA.** It eats mice and other small animals.

The spider in the book *Charlotte's Web* is a **BARN SPIDER.** She is friends with a pig named Wilbur.

The web of this **GOLDEN SILK ORB WEAVER SPIDER** is golden yellow.

The male **PEACOCK SPIDER,** a kind of jumping spider, does a dance to attract a female.

Sitting on a yellow flower, the **GOLDENROD CRAB SPIDER** blends in and is hard to see.

ARIZONA BARK SCORPION

A mother scorpion carries her newborn babies on her back.

A scorpion can live about **SIX YEARS.**

Arizona bark scorpions hide in shaded areas during the day and **HUNT AT NIGHT.**

Have you ever been carried on someone's back?

Arizona bark scorpions do not hatch from eggs. As babies are born, their mother guides them up onto her back. She carries them for about three weeks.

A scorpion has a stinger on the end of its tail. It uses it to sting its prey, such as a cricket. Venom—a sort of poison—flows from the scorpion into the insect.

The venom kills the cricket and turns its insides into liquid—like juice or water. Then the scorpion sucks up its meal.

FACTS

HOME
desert, southwest United States and northern Mexico

FOOD
crickets and other insects

BABIES
up to 35 at a time

PREDATORS
spiders, snakes, mice, peccaries (wild pigs)

SIZE

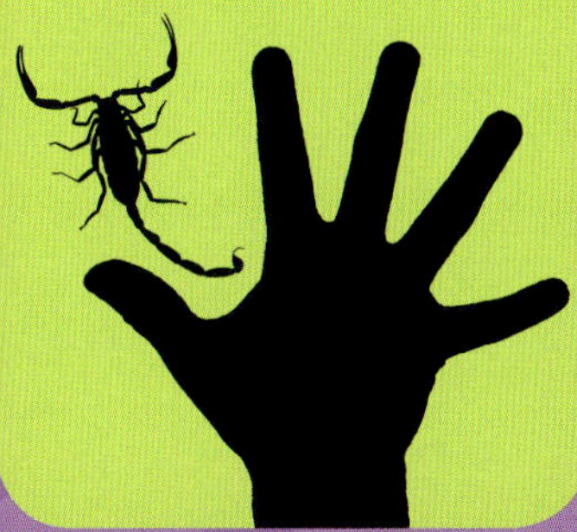

Scorpions are **ARACHNIDS.** They are close relatives of spiders.

DEER TICK

Ticks drink blood.

The deer tick is a parasite. It lives on another animal and gets all its food from it. The animal that a parasite lives on is called the host.

Deer tick larvae hatch from eggs in the late summer. They usually attach to small animals such as mice or birds.

A tick looks different before and after it eats a meal. It is **FLAT AND SKINNY** before it drinks blood. After a meal it is **ROUND AND FAT.**

Do you remember another insect in this book that is a parasite? (HINT: See page 79.)

Adult **DEER TICKS** often live on deer.

After about four days, the larvae drop off the host to the ground. They stay there through winter. In the spring, the larvae become nymphs.

The nymphs attach to small animals, eat for a few days, and drop to the ground again. Now they molt into adult ticks.

Adult male ticks do not eat.

FACTS

HOME
wherever there are deer, in much of North America

FOOD
blood

EGGS
hundreds at a time

PREDATORS
birds, fire ants

SIZE

EARTHWORM

Worms eat dirt.

Earthworms **LOOSEN** and mix garden soil, keeping it **HEALTHY** and a good place for plants to grow.

FACTS

HOME
soil in much of Europe, Asia, and North America

FOOD
leaves and roots in soil

EGGS
about 40 each year

PREDATORS
birds, snails, rats, mice, moles, toads, turtles

SIZE

Earthworms live in soil, or dirt. They crawl through soil and eat it. Bits of leaves and roots in the soil become the worm's food.

The rest of the soil moves out the other end of the earthworm.

Earthworms can tunnel deep underground. At night, they often come to the surface.

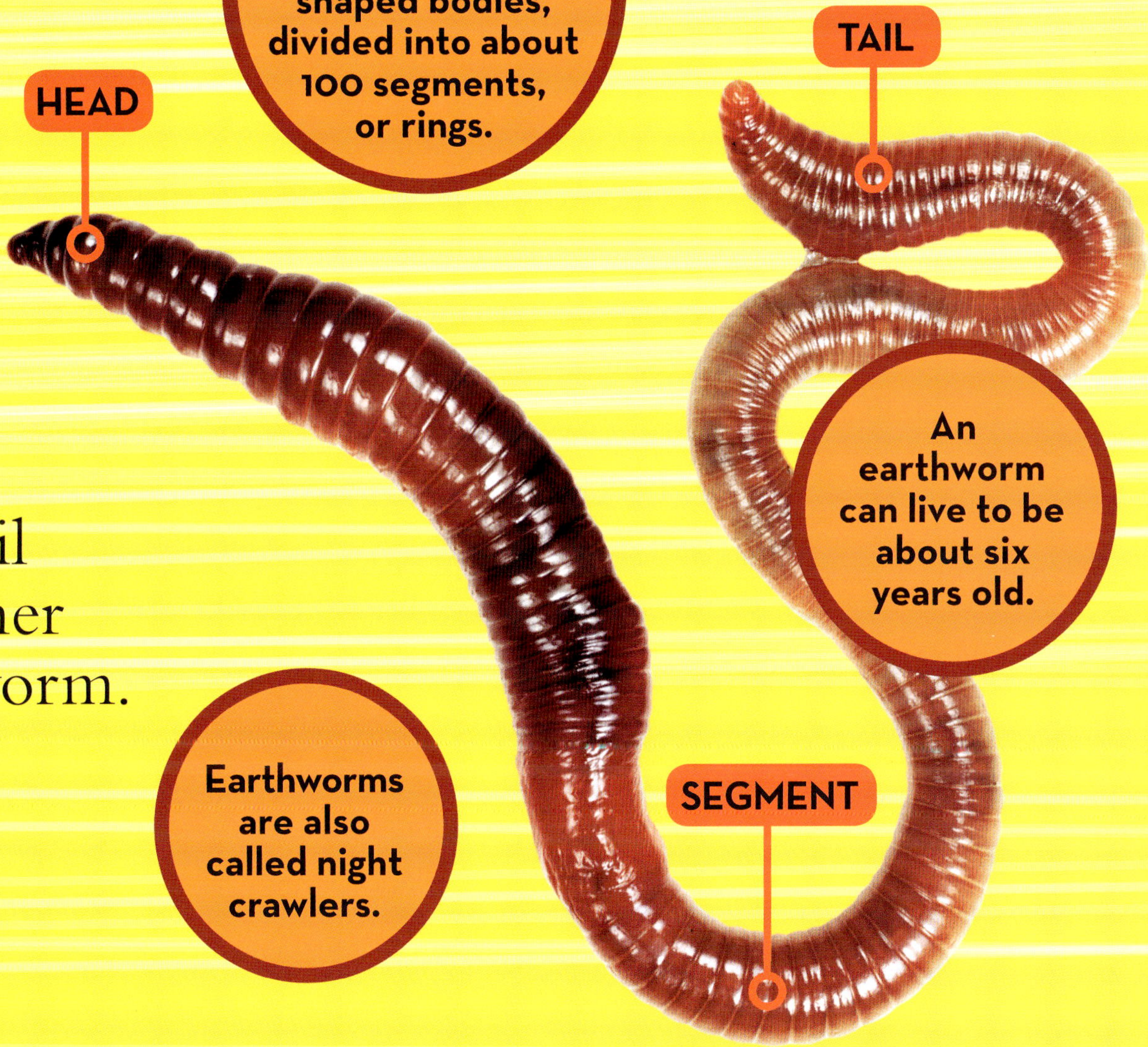

Earthworms are not insects. They have tube-shaped bodies, divided into about 100 segments, or rings.

An earthworm can live to be about six years old.

Earthworms are also called night crawlers.

Have you ever found a worm when you were digging in dirt?

COMMON PILLBUG

These animals are often called roly-polies.

FACTS

HOME
burrows in the ground in wet, dark places, usually in woods and fields in much of North America and parts of Europe

FOOD
rotting plants and animals, fungi

EGGS
several hundred at a time

PREDATORS
birds, frogs, ants, spiders

SIZE

Pillbugs are crustaceans, related to crabs and lobsters. They live on land, though—not in the ocean like crabs and lobsters do.

Pillbugs have an exoskeleton. A pillbug can roll up into a ball. That is why it is often called a roly-poly.

ROLLED UP, PROTECTING ITSELF FROM PREDATORS

UNROLLING

UNROLLING AND READY TO FLIP OVER

A roly-poly has **SEVEN PAIRS** of legs.

A pillbug mother carries her **EGGS IN A POUCH ON HER BELLY.** The young stay there for two months after they hatch.

A pillbug's blood looks **BLUE.**

Which would you rather be, an earthworm or a roly-poly? Why?

Roly-polies are part of nature's cleanup crew. They eat rotting plants and animals, and fungi such as mushrooms.

Pillbug families live together in a burrow underground. The mother and father pillbugs bring food to the burrow for their young.

LET'S PLAY A GAME!

A pattern is something that repeats. The bugs make three patterns in the three rows in this game. Can you say which bug belongs in each of the three empty circles?

2 HARDER

WOLF SPIDER | PILLBUG | EARTHWORM | WOLF SPIDER | PILLBUG

3 HARDEST

PEACOCK SPIDER | DEER TICK | GOLDEN-ROD CRAB SPIDER | DEER TICK | PEACOCK SPIDER

NON-INSECTS

1 EASY

ARIZONA BARK SCORPION

GOLDEN SILK ORB WEAVER SPIDER

ARIZONA BARK SCORPION

GOLDEN SILK ORB WEAVER SPIDER

?

EARTHWORM

WOLF SPIDER

PILLBUG

EARTHWORM

?

DEER TICK

GOLDEN-ROD CRAB SPIDER

DEER TICK

PEACOCK SPIDER

?

PARENT TIPS

Extend your child's experience beyond the pages of this book. Visits to an insect zoo and a butterfly garden are two great ways to continue satisfying your child's curiosity about bugs. Here are some other activities you can do with the National Geographic's *Little Kids First Big Book of Bugs.*

NIGHTTIME BUGS
(OBSERVATION)

On a warm summer evening, hang a white piece of cloth (such as a pillowcase or small tablecloth) on a clothesline or between two poles or sticks placed upright in your backyard. Keep it at a height your child can easily see. After dark, set a lantern or flashlight to shine on the cloth about a foot away. Turn off as many other lights as possible. Wait 20 to 30 minutes for insects to be attracted to the light and land on the white cloth. Talk to your child about the insects you see. Ask her whether there are any species she recognizes from this book. Help her look closely at each one with a magnifying glass and have her describe what she notices.

VISIT ONLINE
(TECHNOLOGY)

School of Ants is a project based at the University of Florida and North Carolina State University. The project involves citizen scientists, such as your child, in making a census of the species of ants found in the United States. For more details, visit this website: *schoolofants.org*

BEETLE-MANIA!
(ARTS AND CRAFTS)

Beetles come in many shapes, colors, and sizes. Encourage your child to make a beetle poster. Have him draw and color a variety of beetles on a large piece of poster board. Add to the fun of crayons and markers by providing sequins, glitter, and other decorations you can find at a craft store. Hang his work of art in his bedroom.

PLANT A BUTTERFLY GARDEN
(BOTANY)

From simply planting a butterfly bush to creating an entire garden filled with butterfly-attracting plants, you and your child can provide attractive food sources for butterflies. Check with a gardening center in your area to find out which plants that grow in your region will attract local butterflies. Have your child help you select and plant the flowers. Include her in caring for the plants. Keep a journal of all the kinds of butterflies you attract. Make a page for each species and help your child draw and color each butterfly visitor to your garden.

GO ON A BUG HUNT
(EXPLORING)

Turn a sunny walk around the neighborhood or through a park into a hunt for bugs. Walk slowly, and

PUSS MOTH CATERPILLAR

even get down on your hands and knees as you look under rocks and logs, dig in dirt, turn over leaves, and check ponds and mud puddles. Encourage your child to keep count of how many bugs he spots. Identify those that you can, but focus on the fun of exploring nature.

BUGGY CARD GAME

(NUMBERS)

Have your child pick twenty of her favorite insects or bugs from this book. Help her draw a picture of each bug on one side of an index card. Number the cards—on the picture side—one through twenty. Shuffle the cards and deal ten to each player. (Add to the number of cards you make if more than two people play.) Each player lays down one card for each turn. Whoever has the card with the higher number gets to keep both cards. The player with the most cards at the end wins.

GLOSSARY

ARACHNID
a group of animals with no backbone (invertebrate), an exoskeleton, two body regions, no antennae, and usually four pairs of legs; includes spiders, scorpions, and ticks

BIOLUMINESCENCE
the light that a living creature produces

CAMOUFLAGE
the ability of an animal to blend in with its surroundings

COLONY
a group of the same kind of animal that lives together

CRUSTACEAN
a large group of animals, such as lobsters and crabs, with a hard outer skeleton, pairs of legs or claws on each segment of the body, and two pairs of antennae

ELYTRON (plural: elytra)
a hard wing cover of a beetle

EXOSKELETON
shell-like outer skin

FOREWINGS
a four-winged insect's front wings

FUNGUS (plural: fungi)
a living organism that is neither animal nor plant, such as mushrooms

HIND WINGS
a four-winged insect's back wings

HOST
the animal that a parasite lives on

INSECT
a group of invertebrate animals with an exoskeleton, three body segments, and one pair of antennae

INVERTEBRATE
animal without a spinal column, or backbone

LARVA (plural: larvae)
the young form of an insect with complete metamorphosis, such as caterpillars and maggots

MAMMAL
a group of vertebrate animals, including humans, that have hair and nurse their young

METAMORPHOSIS
In insects, the change from a young form to an adult. Simple metamorphosis is the change from egg to nymph to adult. Complete metamorphosis is the change from egg to larva to pupa to adult.

NECTAR
a sweet liquid in plants that attracts animals such as insects

NYMPH
an immature insect that goes through incomplete metamorphosis; it looks like a small version of the adult insect

PARASITE
an animal that lives in or on another animal and gets all its food from that animal

PREDATOR
an animal that hunts other animals (prey) for food

PREY
an animal that a predator hunts and kills for food

PROBOSCIS
in an insect, a long tubelike mouthpart through which it drinks liquid food

PUPA (plural: pupae)
a stage in the life of an insect that goes through complete metamorphosis when a larva becomes an adult

REPTILE
vertebrate animals that are covered with scales, and usually slither (such as snakes) or walk on short legs (such as turtles and lizards)

SPECIES
a category, or kind of animal or plant

STRIDULATE
noise made by some insects as they either rub their front wings against their hind wings, or their front wings against their hind legs

THORAX
an insect's body part between the head and the abdomen where the wings and legs are attached

VERTEBRATE
animal that has a spinal column, or backbone

22-SPOT LADYBIRD

CREDITS

HONEYBEE

Abbreviations: AL: Alamy; MP: Minden Pictures; NGC: National Geographic Creative; SCS: Science source; SS: Shutterstock

Cover, irin-k/SS; Back cover, (UP) Dobermaraner/SS; (LO) Paul Harcourt Davies/NPL/MP; Spine, Kim Taylor/NPL/MP; 1, Rolf Nussbaumer/NPL/MP; 2-3, imagebroker/AL; 4, Mark Moffett/MP; 5 (UPLE), Dobermaraner/SS; 5 (UPRT), Lesly van Loo/NiS/MP; 5 (LOLE), FLPA/Nigel Cattlin/MP; 5 (CTR RT), MYN/Clay Bolt/NPL/MP; 5 (LORT), asharkyu/SS; 7 (LE), Manabu Tsutsui/NP/MP; 7 (UP), Stephen Dalton/MP; 7 (LO), Mitsuhiko Imamori/NP/MP; 8-9, Manabu Tsutsui/NP/MP; 10 (UPRT), irin-k/SS; 10 (LOLE), Henrik Larsson/SS; 10 (LORT), motorolka/SS; 11, Cisca Castelijns/Foto Natura/MP; 12 (UPLE), George D. Lepp/Corbis; 12 (UPRT), Dick Poe/Visuals Unlimited, Inc.; 12 (LOLE), Connie Toops; 12 (LORT), Connie Toops; 13 (UPLE), George Grall/NGC; 13 (LOLE), Connie Toops; 13 (RT), AttaBoyLuther/iStockphoto; 14, Wally Eberhart/Visuals Unlimited, Inc.; 15 (LE), Dwight R. Kuhn; 15 (CTR), Dwight R. Kuhn; 15 (RT), Andre Goncalves/SS; 16 (A), FloridaStock/SS; 16 (B), Pete Oxford/MP; 16 (C), Marco Uliana/SS; 16 (D), Mark Moffett/MP; 16 (E), Laurent Conchon/Biosphoto; 16 (F), Piotr Naskrecki; 17 (A), Dr. Morley Read/SS; 17 (B), Piotr Naskrecki/MP; 17 (C), Murray Cooper/MP; 17 (D), Michel Gunther/Biosphoto; 17 (E), Surachan Pramong/SS; 17 (F), nico99/SS; 17 (G), Ingo Arndt/MP; 17 (H), Kim Taylor/NPL/MP; 18-19, szefei/SS; 20, Mark Moffett/MP; 21, Peter Essick/NGC; 22 (UPLE), Edward S. Ross/Visuals Unlimited; 22 (LORT), Alex Wild/Visuals Unlimited, Inc.; 23, James P. Blair/NGC; 24 (UPLE), Mark Moffett/MP; 24 (CTR LE), Piotr Naskrecki/MP; 24 (LORT), Scott Camazine; 26 (LE), Christian Ziegler/MP; 26 (RT), Christian Ziegler/MP; 27, Christian Ziegler/MP; 28 (LOLE), Sandesh Kadur/NPL/MP; 28 (LORT), Susan Thompson Photography/Flickr RF/Getty Images; 28-29, Alex Wild/Visuals Unlimited, Inc.; 29 (UPRT), Robert Sisson/NGC; 29 (LO), Konrad Wothe/MP; 30, Pakhnyushcha/SS; 31 (UP), Gerry Ellis/MP; 31 (LO), Dawna Moore/SS; 32 (LE), Cyril Ruoso/JH Editorial/MP; 32 (RT), Michael Durham/MP; 33, Solvin Zankl/NPL/MP; 34 (UPRT), Alex Staroseltsev/SS; 34 (LE), Apostolos Mastoris/SS; 34 (RT), Anna Sedneva/SS; 35, Gerry Ellis/MP; 35 (LO), Treat Davidson/FLPA; 36 (UPRT), Colin Ewington/AL; 36 (LE), Jef Meul/Foto Natura/MP; 36 (LORT), Michael Durham/MP; 37 (LE), Genevieve Vallee/AL; 37 (UPRT), Bryan E. Reynolds; 37 (LORT), Mary-Anne Meaney; 38, Bryan E. Reynolds; 39 (LE), Bryan E. Reynolds; 39 (LORT), All Canada Photos/AL; 40, Mark Moffett/MP; 41 (UP), Barry Turner/AL; 41 (LOLE), Stephen Dalton/MP; 41 (LORT), Grant Heilman Photography/AL; 42 (UPLE), Satoshi Kuribayashi/NP/MP; 42 (RT), Steve Gettle/MP; 42 (LOLE), Michael Durham/MP; 43 (UP), Mark Moffett/MP; 43 (RT), Pete Oxford/MP; 43 (LO), Murray Cooper/MP; 44-45, Alexander Wild; 46, Kim Taylor/NPL/MP; 46, Pascal Goetgheluck/ARDEA; 47 (CTR), Jef Meul/Foto Natura/MP; 47, Bruce MacQueen/SS; 48 (LOLE), Manabu Tsutsui/NP/MP; 49-49 (UP), Stephen Dalton/MP; 49 (LORT), Mitsuhiko Imamori/NP/MP; 50 (UPRT), Kent Wood/SCS; 50 (LOLE), Rod Williams/NPL/MP; 50 (LORT), B.G. Thomson/SCS; 51 (UP), FLPA/James Lowen/MP; 51 (LOLE), Graphic Science/AL; 51 (LORT), Stephen Dalton/MP; 52, Alexander Wild; 53, Alexander Wild; 54 (UP), Dwight R. Kuhn; 54 (CTR), Scott Camazine/SCS; 54-55 (LO), Gabby Salazar; 54-55 (UP), Steven David Johnson; 56, Inaki Relanzon/naturepl.com; 57, Nick Garbutt/NPL/MP; 59 (A), Bruce MacQueen/SS; 59 (B), efendy/SS; 59 (C), Oz Rittner; 59 (D), Stuart Wilson/SCS; 59 (E), Piotr Naskrecki/MP; 59 (F), Pascal Goetgheluck/ARDEA; 60-61, Jim Brandenburg/MP; 62, Roger Meerts/SS; 63 (UPRT), Stephen Dalton/MP; 63 (LO), Cathy Keifer/SS; 64, Stephen Dalton/MP; 65 (UP), Dobermaraner/SS; 65 (LO), A. Storm Photography/SS; 66 (UP), Nick Garbutt/NPL/MP; 66, Thomas Marent/MP; 66 (UPRT), Ch'ien Lee/MP; 67 (A), Richard Revels/Nature Photographers; 67 (B), Derek Middleton/FLPA/MP; 67 (C), Richard Revels/Nature Photographers; 67 (D), Pete Oxford/MP; 67 (E), Luis Louro/SS; 67 (F), Pete Oxford/NPL/MP; 68, Michael P. Gadomski/SCS; 69, Michael Wheatley/AL; 70 (LE), Robert Henno/Biosphoto; 70 (RT), Mitsuhiko Imamori/MP; 71, imagebroker/AL; 71 (LO), Mitsuhiko Imamori/MP; 72 (A), Derek Middleton/FLPA/MP; 72 (B), Pete Oxford/NPL/MP; 72 (1), Luis Louro/SS; 73 (C), Michael P. Gadomski/SCS; 73 (3), Ch'ien Lee/MP; 73 (2), Luis Louro/SS; 73 (4), Michael Wheatley/AL; 73 (D), Nick Garbutt/NPL/MP; 74-75, Willi Schmitz/E+/Getty Images; 76, Nigel Cattlin/FLPA/MP; 77, Melissa E Dockstader/SS; 78, Kim Taylor/NPL/MP; 79, Vadim Bukharin/SS; 80, Roger Eritja/Foto Natura/MP; 81 (UP), Stephen Dalton/MP; 81 (LO), J. Robinson/Oxford Scientific RM/Getty Images, 82, Grossemy Vanessa/AL; 83 (UP), Michael Durham/MP; 83 (LO), Double Brow Imagery/SS; 84-85, yzoa/SS; 86 (UPLE), Dwight R. Kuhn; 86 (LO), Jeff Greenberg/AL; 87, SuperStock; 88, George Grall/NGC; 89, James H. Robinson/SCS; 90, Gerry Bishop/Visuals Unlimited, Inc.; 91, Paul Harcourt Davies/NPL/MP; 92, Giacomo Radi/ARDEA/ARDEA; 93 (UPLE), Ch'ien Lee/MP; 93 (UP CTR), Thomas Marent/MP; 93 (UPRT), Sebastian Janicki/SS; 93 (LOLE), RGB Ventures LLC dba SuperStock/AL; 94 (A), Brocreative/SS; 94 (B), Andresr/SS; 94 (C), djgis/SS; 94 (D), Le Do/SS; 94 (E), Sanmongkhol/SS; 94 (F), Inga Ivanova/SS; 94 (G), Lesly van Loo/NiS/MP; 95 (A), schankz/SS; 95 (B), George Grall/NGC; 95 (C), yzoa/SS; 95 (D), INSAGO/SS; 95 (E), Sandra van der Steen/SS; 95 (F), Africa Studio/SS; 96-97, Florian Möllers/naturepl.com; 98, Darlyne A. Murawski/NGC; 99 (LE), Paul Whitten/SCS; 99 (RT), Darlyne A. Murawski/NGC; 100-101, Martin Withers/FLPA/MP; 101 (UPLE), Cyril Ruoso/JH Editorial/MP; 102, Mike Lane/iStockPhoto; 103, Kim Taylor/NPL/MP; 104, Mitsuhiko Imamori/NP/MP; 104 (RT), Thomas Marent/MP; 105 (UPLE), Amy White & Al Petteway/NGC; 105 (UPRT), FLPA/Chris Mattison/MP; 105 (LOLE), Frank Jordan/Foto Natura/MP; 105 (LORT), Ch'ien Lee/MP; 106-107, Rolf Nussbaumer/NPL/MP; 108, Adam Jones/Photo Researchers RM/Getty Images; 109, MYN/Clay Bolt/NPL/MP; 110 (UPLE), Larry West/Photo Researchers RM/Getty Images; 110 (UPRT), Mark Romesser/AL; 110 (LOLE), Pete Oxford/MP; 110 (LORT), Andreas Altenburger/AL; 111 (UP), Jürgen Otto; 111 (LOLE), Cisca Castelijns/Foto Natura/MP; 112, Craig K. Lorenz/SCS; 113, Gerold & Cynthia Merker/Visuals Unlimited, Inc.; 114, Dwight R. Kuhn; 115, Picture Press/AL; 115 (INSET), BGSmith/SS; 116, FLPA/AL; 117, Kim Taylor/NPL/MP; 118 (LE), Mitsuhiko Imamori/NP/MP; 118 (CTR), Mitsuhiko Imamori/NP/MP; 118 (RT), Mitsuhiko Imamori/NP/MP; 119, Mitsuhiko Imamori/NP/MP; 120-121 (wolf spider), Henrik Larsson/SS; 120-121 (pillbug), Eric Isselee/SS; 120-121 (earthworm), motorolka/SS; 120, Jürgen Otto; 120-121 (peacock spider), Jürgen Otto; 120 (deer tick), Dariusz Majgier/SS; 120, Dariusz Majgier/SS; 120-121 (goldenrod crab spider), Arto Hakola/SS; 121 (Arizona bark scorpion), Craig K. Lorenz/SCS; 121 (golden silk orb spider), John Dorton/SS; 123, Ingo Arndt/Foto Natura/MP; 124, Jef Meul/Foto Natura/MP; 125, Kim Taylor/NPL/MP; 127, Kim Taylor/NPL/MP

INDEX

Boldface indicates illustrations.

T

V

W

Y

COMMON COCKCHAFER BEETLE

Prepared by the Book Division
Hector Sierra, *Senior Vice President and General Manager*

Nancy Laties Feresten, *Senior Vice President, Kids Publishing and Media*

Eva Absher-Schantz, *Design Director, Kids Publishing and Media*

Jay Sumner, *Director of Photography, Kids Publishing and Media*

Jennifer Emmett, *Vice President, Editorial Director, Kids Books*

R. Gary Colbert, *Production Director*

Jennifer A. Thornton, *Director of Managing Editorial*

Staff for This Book
Priyanka Sherman, *Project Manager*
Catherine D. Hughes, *Project Editor*
Eva Absher-Schantz, *Art Director*
Rachael Hamm Plett, Moduza Design, *Designer*
Lori Epstein, *Senior Photo Editor*
Miriam Stein, *Photo Editor*
Sharon K. Thompson, *Researcher*
Paige Towler, *Editorial Assistant*
Allie Allen, *Design Production Assistant*
Sanjida Rashid, *Design Production Assistant*
Margaret Leist, *Photo Assistant*
Grace Hill, *Associate Managing Editor*
Joan Gossett, *Production Editor*
Lewis R. Bassford, *Production Manager*
Susan Borke, *Legal and Business Affairs*

Production Services
Phillip L. Schlosser, *Senior Vice President*
Chris Brown, *Vice President, NG Book Manufacturing*
George Bounelis, *Senior Production Manager*
Nicole Elliott, *Director of Production*
Rachel Faulise, *Manager*
Robert L. Barr, *Manager*

Dedicated to my sister Stephanie S. Hughes, inspiring champion of all creatures great and small, gardener extraordinaire, talented writer, and my trusted editor.

Hugs and thanks to my youngest bug advisors: Allie, Anna, Elise, Emma, Jack, Jack Edward, Kate, Kaylie, Kurt, Luke, and Wyatt; the students at Grace Episcopal School in Alexandria, Virginia; and the Little Acorn Patch preschool in Kingstowne, Virginia.
—CDH

A special thank-you to Cole Gilbert, Ph.D., Department of Entomology, Cornell University; Andrea Lucky, Ph.D., Department of Entomology and Nematology, University of Florida; and Jiri Hulcr, Ph.D., School of Forest Resources and Conservation, University of Florida, whose time and expertise were invaluable in the preparation of this book.

Acknowledgments
Don Barnard, Ph.D., Research Entomologist, USDA-ARS-CMAVE
Thomas Emmel, Ph.D., McGuire Center for Lepidoptera & Biodiversity, Florida Museum of Natural History
Kim Franklin, Ph.D., Conservation Research Scientist, Arizona-Sonora Desert Museum
Cheryl Hayashi, Ph.D., Department of Biology, University of California Riverside
Claire Install, Conservation Officer, British Dragonfly Society
Eric Rebek, Ph.D., Department of Entomology & Plant Pathology, Oklahoma State University
Garret Suen, Ph.D., Department of Bacteriology, University of Wisconsin-Madison
Nikolai J. Tatarnic, Ph.D., Curator of Entomology, Department of Terrestrial Zoology, Western Australian Museum
David Tarpy, Ph.D., Department of Entomology, North Carolina State University

Thank you to Jack Weible and Blake Thompson for their support throughout the book's progress.

Since 1888, the National Geographic Society has funded more than 12,000 research, exploration, and preservation projects around the world. The Society receives funds from National Geographic Partners, LLC, funded in part by your purchase. A portion of the proceeds from this book supports this vital work. To learn more, visit natgeo.com/info.

For more information, please visit nationalgeographic.com, call 1-800-647-5463, or write to the following address:
National Geographic Partners
1145 17th Street N.W.
Washington, D.C. 20036-4688 U.S.A.

Visit us online at nationalgeographic.com/books

For librarians and teachers: ngchildrensbooks.org

More for kids from National Geographic: kids.nationalgeographic.com

For information about special discounts for bulk purchases, please contact National Geographic Books Special Sales: specialsales@natgeo.com

For rights or permissions inquiries, please contact National Geographic Books Subsidiary Rights: bookrights@natgeo.com

Library of Congress Cataloging-in-Publication Data
Hughes, Catherine D., author.
Little kids big book of bugs / by Catherine Hughes.
pages cm
Audience: 4-8.
Includes bibliographical references and index.
ISBN 978-1-4263-1723-1 (hardcover : alk. paper) -- ISBN 978-1-4263-1724-8 (reinforced library binding : alk. paper)
1. Insects--Juvenile literature. I. Title.
QL467.2.H836 2014
595.7--dc23

2014015520

Printed in China
17/PPS/1 BX